Little Bit of Copyright

Just for Quilters

Dedicated to my mom, Sarita Steinberg Townsend (1940-2008), who both encouraged me to write and to sew,

and to my dad, Robert Joel Townsend (1937-2019) who encouraged my entrepreneurial spirit.

Table of Contents

Preface
A Quick Reference Guide for Quilters

 Why just a little bit of Copyright? All quilters should know the law surrounding creative works, especially if you are posting images online, entering quilt shows, buying patterns, making quilts, purchasing fabric - you get the idea. So, here's just a little bit of copyright to help you navigate the world of creativity.

Want more? We have a more comprehensive book, **Just Wanna Create: Copyright and Fair Use for Quilters, Crafters and Artists.** This is part of a larger series, **Just Wanna,** that includes the titles **Just Wanna Trademark, Just Wanna Patent, Just Wanna Brand, Just Wanna Start, and Just Wanna Contract.** We've also created a **Just Wanna Quilt Notebook**, where you can record your progress, along with copyright and provenance information.

-Ricardo Gonzalez
Editor-in-Chief

Copyright is...

Copyright can be seen as many layers, especially depending on your perspective. Let's take a look to see how we can define copyright.

Copyright is:

- The law behind creativity: I create, therefore I have copyright.
- An economic system: I create, therefore I have the exclusive right to sell my creations.
- A moral system: I create, therefore I should be credited.
- A trade system: I create in the United States, and because of treaties, my creations are protected all over the world automatically.
- A government grant: I create, therefore the government grants me a limited right to control my creation (with exceptions) for a limited time.
- Incomprehensible to most, incompressible, and still a subject everyone worries about. **We're going to change this one right now.**

But creativity is more than copyright.

Copyright is the law that protects creativity.

Creativity

Why do we create? Why do you create? And when we create, how do we feel about the relationship we have to the object now that it exists? How does what we create impact on who we are? On the larger world? On our own personal world?

We create every day. We create to express our love. We create to use our talent to make money. We create to capture moments of our lives. We create to make up new worlds. We create for many reasons.

Our relationship with copyright changes based on the reason for creating.

Personal versus Commercial Use

Copyright interacts with creativity based on a number of factors, the biggest one being personal versus commercial use. If you are creating something for your family, we see very little interaction with copyright law. If you commercialize that same creation, copyright law enters in a big way. This book will help you understand the two spectrums, and the messy in-between middle.

Key Concepts

 Copyright can be complicated. Let's learn a few key concepts that every quilter should know.

First Sale Doctrine: You purchase fabric, a book, or a pattern. You own the physical copy. You can do many things: write in it, resell it, lend it to a friend, make a quilt, and even throw it away. The copyright holder does not control the physical copy *after* first sale.

But:

-This does not include digital copies. First Sale doesn't apply. You can't email or make a copy of a PDF for a friend. There's no First Sale, rather it is seen as a license (like software).

- This also does not allow you to make copies of the book or pattern. You can't copy your purchase and give that copy to a friend. That violates the exclusive right to copy and distribute under the U.S. copyright act.

Techniques: Techniques are not protectable under copyright. You learn to do something in class. You can teach others. You can use it yourself. Techniques and methods are not protectable.

But:

- The expression of the technique is protectable. The handout or book describing the technique is likely under copyright. This includes a recorded class (e.g. YouTube video). This is protectable under copyright

- You can't take notes of a lecture and then publish or post them without permission, or worse, secretly record a session and post it on the Internet. That's covered by the anti-bootlegging laws, and copyright law under the "teacher exception." That's someone else's intellectual property.

Public Domain: Certain elements are available for everyone to use, either because they became part of our common pool of knowledge, or because they are too old to still have copyright protection. Here are some examples:

Our Common Pool

- Shapes, colors, number, fonts (yes!), formulas, common motifs and layouts, textures, and standard basic fabrics (e.g. polka dots, gingham, stripes).
- Traditional blocks like flying geese, log cabin, and the other thousands of versions of repeating blocks.

Old Things

- Anything published before 1924 (this date changes every year).
- Anything first published in the U.S. without proper copyright notice © + date + name before 1989. (Doesn't include foreign works).
- Unpublished works (including quilts) created by someone who has been deceased more than 70 years.

Requirements

 Copyright arises automatically upon creation. That creation is defined as fixed in a tangible medium of expression. So, merely thinking of an idea does not gain protection. Copyright has a few other requirements beyond fixation. Let's take a look.

- Modicum of creativity (something more than just the alphabet or common motifs)
- Human created (called independent creation)
- Creative labor (rather than money or physical labor)

Selection, Arrangement, and Coordination

You take a bunch of things: fabric, common blocks, and an idea to put it all together. Your selection, arrangement, and coordination creates a copyrightable work. You made it. It's yours. And copyright believes that the creative process of taking something from an idea to reality deserves copyright protection.

Idea versus Expression

Ideas themselves are not protectable. They are part of the public domain. We all can use an idea. But the expression of that idea, your version, is protectable.

Spectrum of Infringement: How Different?

You see a quilt online, and you want to make your own version. How different does it have to be? That's hard to say. Here's a rule of thumb: would an average person say, "Hey! That looks like Quilt X." Yours is too close to the original. Use your own creativity to make it truly your own. Pull ideas, but not the selection, arrangement and coordination or the expression from Quilt X. Changing colors isn't enough.

The Concept of Puzzles

We buy a kit. We make it. We don't get a new copyright, even if we change it a little or substitute colors. We are making a copy of the original. We are puzzlers, not creators. We use our skill as sewists. The copyright holder has given us permission to make a copy of their work.

What can we do with our puzzles?

Love them. Give them as gifts. Post them online with proper attribution to the original creator. What about selling them? Your one version, sure. But many copies? Better ask the copyright holder. That's their right to decide.

Aesthetic Non-Discrimination

Copyright doesn't care if your work is good or bad. We don't judge. Really.

Aesthetic Separability and Useful Articles

Copyright doesn't protect useful articles – lamps, blankets, clothing, or recipes, to name a few.

But:

- If you can separate the artistic elements from the useful, copyright will protect it. So, the top of a quilt is distinct from the warmth and functionality. The top and even the quilting are protectable, as long as they are aesthetically separable.

Degrees of Protection

 Copyright breaks us up into categories. If you create something, you have copyright, but only on the creative expression: your original work plus selection, arrangement, and coordination.

Create Something. You get copyright.

Put Proper Notice: Tells the world you are serious about your rights. © Elizabeth Townsend Gard, 2019.

Register Your Work with the U.S. Copyright Office: Tells the world that you will enforce your rights, and could even go to federal court and sue them. You can't sue unless you register your work. You can also, if you win, receive statutory damages up to $150,000 and attorney's fees.

Creative Commons license. You want others to share in your work, and you've told them they can under certain conditions. Go to www.creativecommons.org to learn more.

So, you can tell how serious a copyright holder is in one step: Is there proper notice? If so, respect their work.

A Little Bit of Copyright

Just for Quilters

By

Elizabeth Townsend Gard

Just Wanna Quilt Publications

A LITTLE BIT OF COPYRIGHT JUST FOR QUILTERS

An Imprint of Limited Times Publishing House
New Orleans, LA
www.justwannaquilt.com

Editor-in-Chief, Ricardo Gonzalez

Book design/Layout, Eyeridium, LLC.

ISBN: 978-1-7341271-2-6

Please purchase a copy of the book. The proceeds support the projects at Just Wanna Quilt. If you have suggestions on how to improve them, feel free to email info@justwannaquilt.com. Our books may be purchased in bulk and wholesale for guilds, shops, educational, and business uses. Please contact info@justwannaquilt.com for more information.

First U.S. Edition, October 2019.

About Just Wanna Quilt

Just Wanna Quilt started as a research project at the Copyright Research Lab at Tulane University Law School by Dr. Elizabeth Townsend Gard. It is now a podcast (available on iTunes and other podcast platforms), a community (on Facebook, www.facebook.com/groups/justwannaquilt), and a publishing arm.

Length of Protection

 Copyright does not last forever, although sometimes people feel like it does. Length is important in two respects: what is still under copyright, and how long you can assert your copyright.

New Stuff: Anything created on or after 1978, and anything published after 1989 is automatically protected by copyright without doing anything at all. So, everything around you is pretty much protected.

Old Stuff: As we've discussed, certain things are already out of copyright.
- Published works before 1925 (as of 2020)
- Unpublished works for those deceased before 1950 (as of 2020)

Formalities. For different periods, if formalities were not followed, works came out of copyright earlier.

- No © notice before 1989. Done. It's in the public domain. Note it has to be domestic, not foreign works.

- No U.S. Copyright renewal record for works first published 1924-1963. This is harder. You have to access a special database to see.

The Case of Foreign Works: You should assume they are protected, especially if they are not older than 1944. In some cases, like Germany, everything from 1924 forward is protected. Assume foreign works are protected by U.S. Copyright.

What about the copyright term in Canada? The term in Canada is generally life of the author plus fifty years. So, everything new is protected. And a lot of old stuff is protected too. There are more complicated laws for unpublished works, musical compositions, and other types of works.

Permissible Uses

 Copyright lasts a long time. You do not have to wait until something falls into the public domain to be able to use parts or all of the work. Permissible uses provide different means for engaging with others' copyrighted work(s).

You find an amazing photograph that inspires you to make an art quilt. You want to include lyrics from a song in your quilt. You want to recreate a scene from a film. You want to create a protest quilt using the image of a president. You have so many ideas.

Your own background materials: You shoot the photo. You can do what you want with it. You are creating a derivative work of the original as you transform it into a quilt.

You ask permission: You want to use someone else's photo, and you ask permission to do so.

You rely on fair use: In your new work, you are criticizing or commenting on the original, or you are transforming the work into something entirely different.

Fair Uses

 Fair use is a term that many people know. We're going to go through what it is, and how one applies fair use in a number of situations. Let's understand the structure of the law, Section 107 of the 1976 Copyright Act.

Fair use allows for uses by third parties without permission while the work is still under copyright. Typical uses are criticism, comment, news reporting, scholarship, research, and teaching. Fair use has also been used in technological instances for indexing (think Google searches), time shifting (think DVRs), and parodies (think Saturday Night Live).

Fair use *is not* about using 10% or some other formula to create or differentiate the piece. Instead, it is a balancing test to determine whether the use by a third party is fair to the copyright holder. There are four factors you have to consider.

First Factor: The purpose and character of the third-party use. This is considered very important and can get complicated.

- *Is it a commercial use?* Weighs against third party use. (But not dispositive. Some commercial uses are ok, like parodies)
- *Is it a parody?* Weighs in favor of third party use.
- Non-profit educational use? Weighs in favor of third party use.
- *Transformative?* This is a big one. Have you somehow transformed the original into something else? It is a use different from the original, and somehow you are commenting, criticizing, or transforming in the new work. This is a very important category for artists.

   Art often falls under transformative. When you use a pre-existing art work in a new context, the work may fall under fair use.

Second Factor: The nature of the copyrighted work.

   A work of fiction has greater protection from fair uses, but we still see a lot of fan art and fiction.

   History, directions, and other non-fictional copyrighted works do not get as much protection under the fair use analysis.

Third Factor: The amount and substantiality of the portion used in relation to the copyrighted work as a whole. *How much did the third party take?* This can be complicated too. The amount is both qualitative and quantitative.

> If you take the heart of the work and there's no reason to buy the original, that's not fair to the copyright holder.

> There is no magic number. But think of it this way, if what you are doing is a market replacement that is not a fair use.

> And of course, there is an exception. If you are creating a parody (commenting on a thing in a way that conjures up the thing, again think SNL), you can take the heart of the work – because you need to conjure up the original.

Fourth Factor: The effects of the use upon the potential market for or value of the copyrighted work.

> This is often seen as the most important factor. Is what the third party doing a market replacement or taking away licensing opportunities?

> Note: commenting, criticizing, and parody are not subject to this requirement. The thinking is that the copyright holder would never give permission to have a bad review or be made fun of. So, the fourth factor does not apply.

That's the statute. Now, let's look at some examples.

Examples of fair use:

I write a biography and use quotes from a number of letters and novels of my subject. I use only want I need to in order to comment on the quotes. (Fair use, scholarship)

I take a quote from a poem, and create a quilt using the quote and my interpretation of that poem. (Fair use, comment/criticism, transformative use).

I make a copy from five different books of how each approached the technique of perfect flying geese. I bring them to class to teach different strategies. Because it is a small amount and the lesson is about comparing techniques, that qualifies as fair use. However, if I copy a whole book or a good part, and don't require the students to purchase the book, that is violating factor four and is unfair to the copyright holder.

I use a photograph as inspiration for a quilt. I take the photograph, trace it, and then go about adding textures, colors, and various other elements. I feel like my added work transforms the image into a different story, with different meaning. This is a recent Andy

Warhol case, using a photograph of the musician Prince. The court found the work transformative, when Warhol took a photograph, and made it into his own style.

I am a collage artist. I take bits from a variety of sources, and carefully craft a message that reflects on the original sources. That is fair use.

Fair use is an important tool for artists. If you are using/incorporating someone else's work in your work, stop and think about why. Go through the factors. Does it make sense to call it a fair use? If not, are the parts that you are using in the public domain? If not, are you going to seek permission? If not, you may be infringing.

Finally, we asked our dear friend, Kenny Crews, IP lawyer and expert on fair use for his thoughts on using fair use. He gave us the example of a photograph:

"When you are making a new use, and changing the actual work, your use may be transformative. We have now a handful of photograph cases working their way through the courts. So, we are seeing that courts only are finding transformative work if they create a new work out of the art work that is dramatically different. If it is merely a copy that substitutes for the original that will not be likely seen as fair use. But if that photograph is turned into a very different form of art, then it may be fair use. If you want to commercialize the transformative use, that gets a little bit harder. And we know that hanging a quilt in a quilt show is not considered a commercial use."

Fair use is a powerful and important tool for artists, for our culture, and for our democracy. This is meant merely as an introduction. For more, see the larger book, **Just Wanna Create.**

Just Wanna Quilt Notebook

 The companion book to **A Little Bit of Copyright** is the **Just Wanna Quilt Notebook.** It is designed to help quilters sort through all of the copyright issues and keep track of everything they are doing as they quilt. It includes checklists, copyright information, and fun documentation stuff like the thread you used, ideas, and other things.

Why would you keep track?

For quilt shows: When you enter a show, you will have all of the information you need to fill in the forms.

For your own record keeping: Know which thread you used, what traditional blocks you included and where they came from, and who the quilt was gifted to.

For commercializing your work: Document your process and resources in case you are accused of copyright infringement.

For appraising: Have all of the information needed at your fingertips.

For fun: Who doesn't like to write things down!

For more information about Just Wanna Quilt, go to www.justwannaquilt.com.

Other Just Wanna titles

Just Wanna Quilt Notebook: Record Progress, Copyright and Provenance, by Elizabeth Townsend Gard

Just Wanna Patent: Getting Started by Ricardo Gonzalez (forthcoming December 2019)

Just Wanna Trademark: Legal DIY for Creatives by Elizabeth Townsend Gard

and coming in 2020

Just Wanna Create: Copyright and Fair Use for Quilters, Crafters and Artists by Elizabeth Townsend Gard

Just Wanna Brand: Legal DIY for Our Social Media Age by Ricardo Gonzalez

Just Wanna Start: Legal DIY for Entrepreneurs by Ron Gard

Just Wanna Contract (various authors), edited by Ricardo Gonzalez and Ron Gard

CPSIA information can be obtained
at www.ICGtesting.com
Printed in the USA
LVHW011300041119
636244LV00012B/5357